The You-Turn

by

Lisha R. Williams

Forward by Joe R.

LRW Publishing of Chicago

The You-Turns

Library of Congress
Cataloging in Publication

ISBN 978-0-6151-4964-6

Manufactured in the USA by
Lulu Publishing Company

Published by LRW Publishing
www.lrwpublishing.com

This book is dedicated to

Beatrice Barney

Table of Contents

Acknowledgments

Foreword

A Message to the Readers

Introduction

The Steps to Transformation

About the Author

Acknowledgments

I would like to thank my Heavenly Father for allowing me to take this next step to a higher level. I thank the Lord for being my overseer and faithful friend through the roughest times.

I would like to thank my family for all of their support and guidance, especially my mother and father, Minister Victoria Williams and Alfonzo Williams. Thanks to my grandparents (Johnnie and Eara C. Williams) and my sisters (Lonna Daniels, Linda Morgan and Lanetta Williams) for the love and the many laughs we have shared. I feel so privileged to have all of you in my life. I don't know how I would have survived without you.

I would like to send a special thanks to my aunt, Vernia Hayes, for believing in me when I didn't believe in myself. I couldn't have gotten this far without your words of encouragement.

I want to thank my closest friends who have been like family to me; George and Ramona Boler, Ryan Kersten, Will Frye, Joe R., Phil K., Bertha Tookes and Diane Robinson. Thank you for always extending a hand to me when I needed it the most. You have been a major inspiration to me.

I want to also thank Dr. Eric and Adrienne Barnes for exposing me to great things. Thank you for helping me to blossom during my early adulthood and believing in the success of my future.

I want to thank Robin Beaman; words can not express the love that I have for you. A big thanks to Evangelist T. Baker...I am speechless when it comes to you. You have done so much and I can't say enough to thank you.

Lastly, I would like to thank my church family and their leaders for all of their prayers and support, Apostolic Church of God, Apostolic Faith, Life Changers International Church and Salem Baptist Church.

Thanks to all the MySpace friends for the daily words of encouragement and support. For those who I have forgotten to mention, I apologize. I still want to thank you from the bottom of my heart; may God bless you richly.

Foreword

To say I was surprised when Lisha asked me to write this forward is an understatement. Lisha and I have never met in person; we are chat buddies on the internet but more importantly we are sister and brother in Christ. However, this honor is great because the subject of this book is close to my heart. A pastor once said that 80% of the Christians today are not living the abundant life that the Lord promised us in Psalms 37:4 and in John 10:10, a life where your dreams and desires overflow. That is probably an optimistic estimate since I believe the true percentage is probably less than 5% of those who attend church regularly and who are dedicated to living for Christ; who are open to reaping the abundant life He promises.

In the days of Moses, God specified that there were curses that accompanied disobedience to the Lord; there was a strong element of poverty and lack in these curses. Yet, today, many now praise lack and poverty and actually seek it because they have been taught that poverty and lack is both a virtue and a blessing. The word of God makes it so clear that God is the same yesterday, today and tomorrow. So why would God change lack and poverty from a curse or punishment to a virtue? The answer is that God did not change; over time the church embraced a different teaching. Somehow the passages in the Bible that warned us of making idols of things, money, and possessions were taken to mean that we were to be in lack and poverty while the many passages that spoke of God's generosity were ignored. God loves us and He wants us to be happy and fulfilled, our dreams and desires overflowing in our lives. He is our spiritual Father and like any parent, He wants to bless those of His children who please Him.

I hope reading this book will assist you in realizing how much God loves you. He wants the best for you, so you can live a blessed life, rich in your dreams and desires before the Lord.

Joe R.

Memphis, Tennessee

A Message to the Readers

I would like to take this opportunity to thank you in advance for your support in purchasing this book. My prayer is that it will encourage you and challenge you both mentally and spiritually. Since my last book, I have learned that your biggest blessings come when you are content with what you have. This book is not about how to get rich or a 30-day step to success. It's about believing in YOU and having faith to overcome some of the biggest challenges of life. For instance learning the difference between wanting and needing, God's timing vs. our timing and believing in the midst of doubting. I have always wanted to get to the root of the problem or deal with an issue that can help someone else move to their next level of success. In order for anyone to help another they must have similar experiences. Empathy is the best result for any person to move forward in life. I have learned that the reason God allows us to go through certain situations is not just for us and our own spiritual growth, but to help strengthen and encourage someone else.

My first book, "A Teen's Perspective", meant everything to me because it represented accomplishment and success. Moreover it defined itself as being my struggles in print. My only goal was to guide young people, encourage the lost and to make parents aware of the damaged future that this generation is headed for. We no longer live under the principles, "It takes a village to raise a child". We have allowed our youth to be brainwashed by the negative role models we see on daily television, from music videos to movies. An idle mind is the devil's workshop. If there is nothing in the mind that will sustain them, they are lost. This is why I am so concern about the well-being of our youth. Who will be the one to stand firm and become a leader? Where are our future doctors, lawyers and working professionals? When I talk to young people they are so amazed by athletes, celebrities and so forth. It's not just the money and the bling they are so focused on. They are looking at the fame and so many young people are thirsty for attention. Who is willing to stand in the gaps for our youth? Who is willing to change their hearts and minds? Who is willing to provide the attention they need?

When I decided that I would write this book, I knew that just by looking back on how far the Lord brought me it would give me goose bumps. Overall I knew that my life was going to turn around for the better, but I couldn't get a grip on how it would come about. I began to see things differently and I was beginning to mature spiritually. I knew that as I got older that my past would mean something totally different to me now. Though I am amazed at how God brought me through my trials of the past and how He is keeping me today, I can see the patterns of deliverance, the growth of spiritual awareness, the depth of God's blessings and wisdom that only He could grant me. I have finally come to that point of my life where I know that God has a purpose for me and all I have to do is seek Him. "Seek first the kingdom [of God] and all His righteousness will be given unto you." (Matthew 6:33 - NIV) It is His timing and His plan that will keep me on the straight and narrow.

The one thing I pray that you receive from this book is nothing more than divine revelation, encouragement and strength. I pray that it will equip you and make you ready for the future because the best is yet to come. God bless you.

Introduction

He has given me strength to endure, peace that passes all understanding and joy everlasting. He has given me all that I needed and much more. Who is He? He is my Heavenly Father. I thank God for his loving arms around me. I am elated to know that He has never left me nor forsaken me even when I felt like I couldn't go on. During times of great trials and tribulations, I didn't understand the purpose of the various tests I had to endure. It took time for me to realize that "faith is the substance of things hoped for and the evidence of things not seen". (Hebrews 11:1 NIV) I am at the point where I am ready to move forward and there's no looking back. Everything that the enemy has stolen from me, I am about to receive it back seven times greater than before. This is the time for healing and deliverance. It's time for a breakthrough and a major release. It's time to get out of your comfort zone and answer the calling that was spoken over your life.

"You-Turn" is nothing more than transformation. When you are transformed, you begin the process of the 180 degree turn. That's when people decide that nothing can steer them away from their dreams of success. "Don't be conformed any longer to the ways of the world but be transformed by the renewing of your mind. Then you will be able to find what God's perfect will is. "(Romans 12:2 NIV)

So many people have dreams that they have not fulfilled due to fear and lack of self-confidence. This book will challenge you to take that leap of faith despite your circumstances. It's about realizing who you are and the fact that life will have many ups and downs. By staying focused on your dream and being reminded that no obstacle can stand in your way, you have a tendency to believe that you can turn your life around and go for it.

You can do all things through Christ who strengthens you. (Phil. 4:13 KJV)

***

Dear Lord,

I come before You with heaviness in my heart. I feel broken and torn, to some degree confused, for I don't know what steps I should take, which direction I should go. I am trusting and leaning on Your everlasting arms. I come with faith greater than the grain of a mustard seed. I believe that what's for me is for me. You have placed this dream within me, so I ask that You water this seed and let it flourish about. I believe in You and what You can do.

Lord, I have allowed my flesh to dictate my character. I am at the point of release. I surrender and give myself fully unto You. I know that new beginnings are arising and a brand new me is about to surface. A totally purged and purified vessel has been released to be used by the One, who is able to keep me from falling and to present me faultless before the throne.

Thank you Lord for listening to me when no one else would listen... Thank you Lord for the transformation and the renewing of my mind, the rejuvenation of my spirit... Keep my eyes on the cross, the crown and the throne. I know that great things are about to happen because I believe.

In Jesus' name...Amen

The Steps to Transformation

1. Be proud of who you are. Don't let anything tear you away from your dream.

2. Be humble. Never forget where you came from. Learn from your history because history repeats itself.

3. Teach great values to those who look up to you and generations to come will benefit.

4. Trust and believe in your dreams. Don't let them fade away by your fears, by your race, by your gender or by your physical disadvantage.

5. Love those who hate you. Cherish those who have raised you. Embrace those who pray for you.

6. Set goals and strive to meet them. Always expect great things.

7. Believe in God, then in yourself; believe in the possibilities that you will make it against all odds.

8. Give back and reach out to those who are seeking a way out.

9. Express yourself and find your passion. Be bold in your beliefs, your dreams and your life. Remember to never let doubt overshadow you.

10. Last but not least, remember to always keep God first in all that you do. Have faith and trust that you will overcome any circumstance or obstacle.

Chapter 1

IF I KNEW THEN WHAT I KNOW NOW

Have you ever looked back on something and wished that you could do it all over again? Have you ever been embarrassed about something and can't seem to let it go? Have you ever seen someone from your past that hits a sore spot? Sure, there are plenty of times I felt that there should be a planet out there just for me, but it's not quite like that. I had to learn how to face things even when it hurt me. I had to stop running from everyone who tried to attack me. I had to face my fears and challenges no matter how hard they were. It's called life.

The movie "It's A Wonderful Life" is one of my all-time favorite movies due to its spiritual outlook. It deals with the same issues we face on a daily basis. For instance, how we fear failure and how we want to throw in the towel when things don't quite go the way we planned. George Bailey, the main character, found himself in one dilemma after another, mainly in regards to his finances. Though what George didn't realize was his value to his family and friends, how they depended on him and how he played such an accentual role within their lives. He showed his love and compassion toward helping others. With George not realizing the importance of his very existence, he thought that his life was meaningless. He felt depressed, hopeless and worthless. George felt that all hope was gone but God sent him a guardian angel named Clarence. George wished that he had never been born and

Clarence allowed for his wish to come true. Clarence wanted George to see what the world would be like without his accomplishments being met.

George had many accomplishments after the passing of his father. He had inherited his father's wealth, took over his father's banking business, got married to the woman of his dreams and had three beautiful children. He even invested money on building affordable housing for the less fortunate and worked with the people in the community. You would think to yourself, "How in the world did George feel that he had no purpose in life?" As crazy as it may sound, George represents all of us. We have success knocking at the door of our hearts and because of one mishap we give up. You may get a promotion on your job because your boss thinks highly of you. So with this promotion you receive a financial increase, a bonus, a respected position of authority and a matching donation to your 401(k). He does this for you because he knows that you are worthy and more than capable to do the tasks that's required of you. Yet it's because of one person on the job, who dislikes you, finds a glitch in some of your work or disrupts your plan, you get discouraged. This is how the enemy operates, by using people through jealous behavior. The same if you are in school and you receive top-notch grades. The teacher requests that you be accelerated to a more advanced level because your teacher knows your ability of achievement. You may be moved to another position in the church because the pastor sees a greater need for you in another auxiliary. We must not be afraid of change and trust in God when He takes us out of our comfort zone.

Life has so many bumpy roads, twists and turns, but these things happen to us to perfect us. God's plan for our lives is so uncertain, though we must be willing to trust in His Will. When we trust in God for things to happen and pray for certain things, they may not happen right away. This is one of the many things that discourage us when it comes to success. We become gullible to negative thoughts and we adhere to what the world thinks of our dreams and ambitions. There are many individuals who would laugh and mock you because you believe that God will bring you out of your circumstances and into your promised land.

As a prime example of unwavering faiths, the Bible tells us about a man named Job. Throughout it all, Job trusted in God through some of the worst conditions and he had suffered greatly. The enemy sent forth Job's so-called friends with misguided advice, telling him that what he was going through was because of wrongdoings of his past. Even Job's wife, out of anguish, told him to curse God and die. Wow, that's encouraging don't you think? (I'm just joking) Though God had his hand on Job and made him honorable in His sight. Job was only tempted because God allowed it to happen to prove a point to the enemy, that he would never receive the victory over any of God's chosen ones. Even though God doesn't have to prove a point to anyone, He used Job in the scriptures to allow His people to know that He is always on the throne. In Hebrews 13:5 it states "...I will never leave you nor forsake you." If it's in the Word of God then it's true.

There are so many faithful servants in the Bible who can encourage us in this day and time. Life in itself has many challenges but we must dance to the music that is played for us.

Journal Quotes: *As I was going through some of my old journals I became encouraged by some of the things I was going through. I saw how far the Lord had brought me and I also noticed some of the bad habits of negative thinking starting to resurface.*

June 25, 2004 - "What's your level of Faith?" This is what I've learned to ask myself when crisis arise. I have learned to ask God for radical request because he will bless me radically. I have learned to never underestimate God's power.

June 26, 2004 - My expectations in life may seem so far fetched, as if there's no purpose for living. Though I know I have a purpose, I just don't have any idea of what the future holds for me. I want my life to count for something. I want to prioritize my life goals and align them with God's will. I know that I'm here for a reason and only for a season.

June 27, 2004 - "What is Faith?" Faith is an act of believing. What if you believe in something and it never happens? Does that mean you lack in faith? No, of course not... That means that what we wanted, was not what we needed. Though in the Word of God, Luke 11:9 tells us to "ask, and it shall be given unto us." The Lord will bless us with the desires of our hearts, yet he shall also supply all of our needs. God doesn't spoil His children rotten but He disciplines us. He molds us and shapes us for perfection in His sight...not by men.

July 9, 2004 - I've come to realize that without God all things are difficult. With God all things are possible.

July 19, 2004 - My prayer is for the Lord to guide my walk, by taking over my thinking and letting my desires be met by His Will.

August 8, 2004 - Even though faith is an act of believing, it's better said then done. We live in a time when so many are dishonest but you must remember to put your trust in God and He will sustain you.

My friend, Robin Beaman, is more of a mentor to me then anything else because she always has the most encouraging things to say. It was her idea for me to have a special kind of journal called, "A Dream Journal". In this journal I wrote all of my future goals that I would like to achieve. It's like a blue print. My mother has always told me to write things down so I'll always have a reference guide. If you write your goals down, you are breaking ground and getting the foundation prepared. This is the only way to begin building your dream. The Dream Journal is my reference guide. When I read my journals, I am always amazed at how encouraging I can be at one point and then I am so discouraged the next. It's like an emotional roller coaster ride. One moment you're on the top of your joy, the next moment you dive into the deep end.

If you don't have a journal, I RECOMMEND YOU GET ONE. Believe me it's the best investment you can make to prepare you for the success of your dream. Once you get your journal, write your dreams and goals down and then pray over it. Ask God to hear your needs and grant you favor that it will come to pass. If it's in His Will for you to have what you request of Him, He will grant it to you. I don't look at God as being some wonderful genie in a bottle, but I see Him as my Heavenly Father who will bless me, by His Will and by His timing. You may ask yourself, "Why do my dreams seem so outrageous?" We serve a God who's El Shaddai, the God who's more than enough. I dream big because I know that God blesses in abundance.

My dream is to be a servant of God, a witness among men, a testimony for the lost and a living proof for unbelievers. In Hebrews 11:1 it states "Faith is the substance of things hoped for and the evidence of things not seen." I have faith in my dreams that they will come to pass as long as they are in alignment with God's plan for my life. I may dream something that I may believe is big but God may have something bigger and better in store.

In the beginning stages, my top priority was to accomplish confidence in myself, so that I could believe I am worthy of success. I began to feel encouraged to move the mountain of defeat because it didn't play any role of importance in my life. It doesn't play a role in the hearts and minds of anyone who loves and believes in the Lord. Acting in faith is believing in God's Word. When you believe, then you can achieve. The Word of God says, "Life and death is in the power of the tongue." What comes out of your mouth is what comes out of your heart. You can verbally attack yourself without being aware that you're doing it. Stay focused to what the Lord is calling you to do because He is the One that places the dream within you.

Encourage Yourself to Stay Focused

Doing the unexpected may seem like doing the impossible, but you must leave the impossible in the hands of the Lord God makes the impossible seem so easy when you just cast your cares to Him. For instance, take a sheet of paper at write down in a column all the things that you want to accomplish; your dreams and your goals. In the second column, write down all the things that are stopping you from reaching your highest potential of making that dream become a reality. Most of you will come up with the conclusion that your finances are your major stumbling blocks because you are looking toward your current living situation. Instead, I want you to look outside your budgets and tell yourself the truth. The only thing that's stopping you from success is you. That second column is nothing more than excuses. Think of all the doors of opportunity that awaits you...think of all the possibilities you have. God has given you only one life to live and what you do in this lifetime really matters.

We have a family friend named Gary, who has a great gift as an artist. His work is so profound. The colors come to life and the drawings are so bold that it appears you are sitting right in the painting. I asked my mother why he never had an art show. She told me that he didn't think that he was good enough to have one. We are our worst critics. We can see things in other people that we can't see in ourselves. We could tell ourselves I don't have the look to be a model, I don't have the time to go back to school, I don't have a car to get to that seminar that'll help me start my own business. They are all excuses because many of us fear success. If you know that you have the ability to do something or you have the talent...go for it.

I am not the one for "reality" shows, yet there is one show that I look at periodically, which is American Idol. The people who try out for the show all have one thing in common; they have that dream of becoming a star. This is the perfect example of dreamers reaching toward their goal. They can all picture themselves being on stage in Hollywood doing their thing. Though, Simon has to put a reality check on a lot of people. Many of them don't have the talent to perform. If Simon doesn't criticize them now, the public will do it later. This is not to say that some of these people can't have vocal lessons, which will train their voices so they will be able to use them properly. I mentioned the American Idol show because we will all receive some form of rejection. That's a part of life. When someone says no, that's not so you can feel defeated.

One of my mentors, Minister T. Baker once told me that, "Delay doesn't mean denial". It happened to me with my first book signing event. I had waited for weeks for this book signing to come. I was in my teens when I put my first book together and I was so happy when that time had arrived for me to make my grand appearance. Announcements were made, invitations were sent out and some of my biggest role models were going to be there. I got to the bookstore and saw my poster in the window and my book on display. A beautiful table was being set for where I was to sit and sign. Once I got there I was told that my book signing was cancelled. I turned around to walk away and I was devastated and embarrassed. I couldn't even take it much longer to the point that I just cried. I kept thinking to myself, if I were a celebrity they would have never done this to me. I wasn't a well-known author and I knew that things like this are always bound to happen. I had spent my very last on a taxi to get to the bookstore and all I had to look forward to were my books to sell.

A woman named Evangelist Diane Kendricks saw how distraught I was. I didn't know her and she didn't know me but something inspired her to walk up to me and hug me. She embraced me as if we were long time buddies and told me that the Lord sent her to me. She didn't know about anything that was going on, nothing whatsoever. After I stopped crying, I told her what had happened. She looked at me, smiled, and then asked, "Can I buy one of your books?" I looked at her with a very puzzled look because I was so shocked. When she purchased a book I became so excited, not to mention there was my carfare back home. Even with this one blessing, the Lord wasn't through with me yet. Only minutes later my mother told me that more people wanted to purchase books. The Lord can mend a broken heart. What the devil meant for evil, the Lord turned it around for the good. Sometimes we don't understand why things happen but it's definitely because the Lord wanted it to happen that way. I felt defeated and I even became a little selfish but once I humbled myself, that's when the Lord began to bless. I was blessed with strength and encouragement.

Lisha R. Williams

Chapter 2

DREAMS AREN'T SO HARD TO COME BY

I am just like anyone else; I have high hopes about a goal that I would like to achieve, after so long the thrill vanishes. I have learned that God is in control no matter what. If you have a dream or goal that you want to achieve, you must take it to the Lord in prayer. It may seem absurd, but there are times when your dreams may not be in alignment with God's Will for your life. You may have a talent in one thing but God sees a greater talent in something else; something that will allow you to reach other people. You may have a desire to do something in the United States but the Lord may want you to do something in Brazil. You never know what God has in store for your life.

Oprah once stated, "God can dream a bigger dream for you than you can dream for yourself". If anyone can be a witness to that statement is definitely Oprah. We must remember that she didn't become a top sensation overnight but it was in God's timing. I am quite sure that she wasn't aware of the blessings God had in store for her while growing up in the South. Even with many obstacles to face during a time of segregation and racism, there were only two choices to make. Those two choices were faith (victory) or failure (defeat). God will bless you more abundantly and He will have your cup overflowing. The Lord will bless you in abundance so that you may be able to be a blessing to others. Even Oprah gives in abundance because she receives in abundance.

I used Oprah as an example because a variety of people can relate to her story. The world titles this kind of lifestyle as "Rags to Riches". You may have dreams that are grand, but keep in mind that everyone will not become a world renowned icon. God has positioned people in many different areas. There are many people who have testimonies just like Oprah, who are not celebrities. What about the successful doctor from your old neighborhood that was given only six-weeks of life to live at birth? What about the successful TV anchor who grew up in the same low-income housing program as you? There are so many different people, with so many different dreams, all around the world. The endless stories are all answered by faith. God can use all people of all races and nationalities.

You have to capture your heart's desire and really dictate what your dream is. Think about why this dream is so important to you. What do you desire of the Lord? You may have a dream to build a brand new home, with new furniture and beautiful interior decor. You may want to begin a Christian bible study. You may want to begin a home-based business. You may want to open up a business within your community. You may want to do something for the children in your neighborhood and surrounding areas. Whatever it may be, pray on it and ask for direction and leadership abilities. Pray that the Lord will send the right people to make your dream possible.

So many times I hear people talk about "free will" and doing things there own way. Been there, done that. If you do whatever you want to do, you will easily set yourself up for a complete disaster. You can not do it alone. When you pray for your dreams to become a reality, things just happen to fall into place and doors of opportunity will begin to open. The Lord will send the right individuals you need to help you.

I admire one of the most encouraging men around, John C. Maxwell, a well-known author who wrote the book "Dream Work Makes the Teamwork." He discusses in full detail why we need others to aid us on our missions and why we are not to take things into our own hands. You need the help of others and you need to learn from others. How can you start a business without any guidance from other successful entrepreneurs? How can you build a brand new home without any knowledge of real estate? You need other people to network; that's why it is important to pray for the Lord to send those people to you. I have learned that all successful people, whether they're corporate, entrepreneurs, etc, had someone to boost them up for encouragement. God sends certain people into your life and moves others out of your life for a reason. The Lord begins to prepare you for your next destination, that higher level of success. It's not coincidence that these people happen to arrive but they are all motioned by God's hands. Our flesh, by natural instincts, wants to cling onto people and things that hold us back of our promised land. One of the most crucial, damaging, heartbreaking things about people and there dreams is their level of confidence. There are so many people who make excuses for why they are unable to do what the Lord has called them to do. I am reminded of Moses and his many excuses to why he shouldn't be the one to lead the people out of bondage. He made all kinds of excuses but the Lord used him mightily. God even sent Aaron, his brother, to translate for him. There was an extreme lack of confidence on Moses' behalf.

Intimidation is another stumbling block for many people. Some of us fear success because we are afraid of what someone else will say or think. Don't worry about what others are doing and saying because you have to stay focused to what your dream is. That's the only way you'll be able to move forward. When you are driving a car, you aren't looking at the people on the side of you. You aren't even paying attention to the people who you have passed up. You are paying attention to the person in front of you for any sudden and unexpected occurrences. You have blind spots that you must check when switching lanes and you have side mirrors that give you all kinds of warning signs. Stay in your lane. Don't linger around in lanes that will change the road to your success. Stay focus to the things that are ahead of you and that's already in motion. Put your foot on the breaks only when it's necessary to do so.

What gives you a boost?

Think of some recreational or extra-curricular activities you like to do that encourages you to push yourself to the maximum. What gives you that kick to move forward and motivates you to go to the next level? It may be your kids, it may be music or motivational tapes and books, no matter what it is, it has to be something that will push you to that point of living your life to the fullest.

The thing that keeps me going is music. It may drive the people around me nuts, though it gives me my daily boost and it allows me to dream. I love the Christian pop artist TobyMac because he puts all of his dreams and desires in his music. I also love classical music and I love to listen to the most popular pieces from Bach to Beethoven to Sebastian to Tchaikovsky. I call this my "music of reflection" and every time I hear it, it allows me to think of how I can set this or that goal and stick to it. I have learned so much about this thing called "life". I have come to realize that 80% of what we fear never happens and 20% of what we say about ourselves is not true. I am not a psychologist so of course my percentages may be off, but the question that ponders at me the most is, "How can we live the full potential of our lives if we don't act on it?" I always think about my ancestors who were so strong and fought their way to liberty. Everyday is a struggle to succeed and the only way you can do it is by moving as the wind blows. Take each day as if it were your last. I am thankful for the opportunity to see another day because I know that life is a gift from God. I know that every breath that I take is a miracle. I know that every step that I make is another step closer to my dreams being met.

Soar Like the Eagles

I believe that if you want to succeed, you will have to go where only the eagles soar. You have to surround yourself with people who are like you; people who are going places and doing great things. Negative energy can rub off on a person quicker than the positive energy. Why? When people are negative, they tend to think of things that are practical and logical. They are not creators or inventors, nor will they ever be leaders because they always follow in the shadows of someone else. They are the type of people who will give you all the reasons of why you can't do what you dream of doing. Oppose to a positive person who is willing to give you a hand where they can, negativity has a way of easily persuading a person by using the possibilities of something going wrong. They are the ones who can not see the vision of one's

Lisha R. Williams

dream. For instance, I have heard people say that they can't do something they like because of their skin color, the ethnicity or sometimes even their gender. Life should be controlled by the person who is living it. No one should be able to dissuade you of doing something that God has placed in your spirit to do. Though don't throw away good advice. Don't mistake someone's helpful advice with a negative person's complaint. When a person gives advice, they are not trying to steer you away you from you dreams but they have other alternatives to help your dream become a reality. One thing that I can say in pure confidence is nothing can stop one's potential to succeed in life but that person.

Fight the Good Fight of Faith

I came a long way and the best thing is the Lord isn't done with me yet. He has a lot of blessings in store for me. I have learned that no matter what it is that we face in life, the prayers of the righteous avail much. Always remember when you let God take over the wheel, the enemy will try to reach for the brakes. Let go and let God. Be ready to make the transition to a totally new path that God has paved for you.

I adore my oldest sister Lonna, being that she is the Human Resources Manager for the largest retailer in the world; she is use to hearing complaints and excuses from people on a daily basis. With her being a ten-year cancer survivor, absolutely nothing can stop her from believing. No one can take her dreams away from her. She doesn't take life for granted.

Lonna feels that sometimes people can get discouraged when they share their dreams with other people because they don't always buy-in from those who don't share their vision. When I spoke to Lonna regarding this subject of sharing the vision, she stated that, "One can establish a broader network of people who can help accomplish goals...sharing dreams can gain open doors to possibilities one never knew they had."

Journal Quote 2006

What's holding you back from making the best decisions of your life? Why are we so afraid to confront adversity? Why are we so bogged down and afraid to move out of our comfort zones?

It's so refreshing to know that when you have a dream (the impossible dream) you can always count on God to direct your path. Of course, it's the 21st century and who wants to talk about God? Better yet, who wants to acknowledge His existence? It's not cool and it's so old fashioned. Let me tell you my friend, you have never been more incorrect in your life. To do anything successful without God is foolish. Always put God first...you may not believe it when you hear it but only God can unleash your power within. Unleash the power of greatness and a peace of mind. Unleash your greatest talents and greatest motivations.

So I challenge you today to say a prayer. Silently or aloud...He can hear them both. Reunite yourself with Him. Let Him know that you have not forgotten Him. Let him know that you have put Him first above everything...above your job, your marriage, your relationships or your material things. Pray for direction that God will lead you to the right way of success. Do you trust Him...do you believe?

Chapter 3

SPILLING THE BEANS ABOUT YOUR DREAM

So many people have broken and shattered hearts because they have revealed their dreams to people who didn't believe that it was possible to achieve them. One thing that has a tendency to hurt me the most is the lack of support people show to others, especially those from the church. My mother has told me on several occasions, "Not everyone in the church is saved and not every saved person is delivered." Sometimes people get jealous when they hear about your dreams, your blessings and even your success stories. They begin to compare themselves to you and see where they measure up. These are the type of people who prefer not to see you get ahead in life. They are the ones who refuse to see you happy. It makes them feel intimidated to know that someone is going places and doing great things. Sometimes the blessings that you receive from the Lord are what others want for themselves. In every way possible, these individuals will try to take your blessing away from you or stop you from getting it all together.

One of the many reasons why you can't tell some people about where you've been and where you're going is because many will doubt you. Some people are known for carrying a negative spirit by laughing at you and mocking your dream. That's only because they're looking from the natural [carnal] and not the supernatural. This kind of negative feedback that comes from negative people usually discourages a dreamer from dreaming or

breaks their level of confidence. People that hold a negative
tongue against you will begin to make you focus on your finances,
your current living situation, your troubled kids or your fragile
marriage. They will begin to tell you that your dreams are
impossible by saying, "luck of that kind will never pass your way".
First of all, the one thing they have correct about your dream is
that it's definitely impossible. That's why it's in God's hands and
not yours. Secondly, it's not about luck, it's called a blessing.
When you tell someone about your dream and they give you a
negative response, learn how to turn a deaf ear. Trust and believe
that your dream will come to pass.

I interviewed a dear friend of mine Alicia, who happens to be one
of the managers for a collection and dispute resolution group.
Alicia feels that sharing your dreams with others is not the real
problem but believing in your heart that they'll come to pass,
despite the negative responses received from others.

Alicia said, "I believe you should share your dreams with
significant others, but the final decision should be yours.
Communication is the key to any relationship. Our dreams are
part of who we are. If we are striving to have authentic
relationships we need to share who we are. The key is not to
expect everyone to feel the same way as you do about your
dreams. Some people are dream killers and don't realize it.
Sometimes the intent is to protect because they can't see it for
you. The intentions are good, but the end result can be
discouraging. Others, for selfish reasons don't want you to leave
them behind so they sabotage your dreams. In summary, you can
get the opinions of others who may have wisdom or insight, but
make your decision for yourself. You only get one life to live and

you can't go back and blame anyone else for it...if I could've, would've... but yourself."

I asked Alicia did she believe that she could have gone further in life if she didn't have children, wasn't married, went to a certain college, had more money or lived in another location. She told me, "On the surface it may seem like if only I had more money or a college degree, things would be better, but I believe all things are possible through Christ and that he knows exactly where he wants you to be placed. Our steps are ordered, so whatever we experience in our lives is for a reason. Maybe you don't have more money because you haven't proven yourself to be an effective steward with what you have now and God wants you to learn that lesson before blessing you with more. Maybe you are married to learn from you spouse. Maybe you didn't go to college when you were younger because you could not have appreciated the experience at that time, or the teacher, classes, program, etc required to fulfill your purpose were not available at that time."

Alicia knows that whatever it is that she desires of the Lord, it would be granted to her because she has to go before the Lord with a petition of faith and ask for her double-portion blessing. Alicia mentioned to me that when she looks back over her life the only explanation for so many blessings is Christ. She says, "I know that I am a Child of God and He wants what is best for His children." It's all about believing that the Lord Jesus Christ is the same yesterday and today and forever. Hebrews 13:8

Negativity vs. Constructive Criticism

Another thing you must realize is that people who care about you may give you some pointers that may just help you along the way. In this instance, please don't consider them to be negative. This is what "constructive criticism" is and everyone needs it every so often. Constructive criticism is when someone leads the way to help you stay focused on your goal. There are times that we may have a dream to do something that is not the will of God or it may not lift of the ground without proper protocol.

I have three older sisters that look after me solely because of love. They know my heart and the things that I want to accomplish, so they'll give me suggestions on how I can improve something that I want to do. At times, I just need for them to tell me how to make my dream work for me and for others that's involved with it. Yes, there are times that I don't focus on one particular project and I begin shifting to other areas that are not meaningful. Once again, my sisters are there to steer me in the right direction so I won't get off course. I always leave the table out for comments, suggestions and constructive criticism because I know that it will help me in the long run. I will admit that I may not like it at first but eventually it will sink in and I will finally see the big picture.

Joseph and His Dreams

The Bible speaks about a young man named Joseph, who was the son of Jacob and Rachel. He's best-known for being the dreamer and the interpreter of dreams. He was the most-loved and shown much favor out of the twelve sons of Jacob. Joseph's story was even portrayed in a Broadway musical a few years ago titled

"Joseph and the Amazing Technicolor Dreamcoat". The directors of this musical made the story of Joseph pretty comical but in all truth, Joseph is another person who represents the vast majority of all of us. How long are we willing to wait on our blessing from the Lord? How long are we willing to stand still and let God take care of the impossible on our behalf? How long are you willing to hold on just a little longer for the Lord to grant the desires of our hearts? Just like Joseph's brothers, there will be many who will get angry and jealous of you.

Joseph remembered that he had a special place in Jacob's heart, even during the long period of separation from him, just as you have a special place in the Father's heart where He wants to bless you more abundantly. He states that in John 10:10, "The thief [enemy] comes to steal, kill and destroy, but I come that they may have life and have it more abundantly."

The trials and tribulations that Joseph had to endure made him stronger and prepared him for leadership as Pharaoh. Joseph saw his own dream over and over again but he never stopped dreaming. Even in bondage he was granted favor among men but it never dawned on him that he'd have to go through trials in order to become one of the greatest leaders in history. How would he have been able to relate to slavery and the brutality of slave masters if he would have never gone through it? How would he understand betrayal if he had never been betrayed? He wasn't born into royalty but was granted favor from the Lord and placed in royalty. The Lord never left him so therefore He will never leave you.

Honesty

One of the most inspiring minister's I know is Bishop Arthur M Brazier, the pastor of the Apostolic Church of God in Chicago. I am inspired by him because he uses real life situations to encourage you. I love listening to people who've gone through situations I can relate to because I have found great comfort and trust in people who are honest. Some have their on views of what honesty really is, but so many people lack honest lives due to egotistical reasons. Many times it could be pride that puts a speed bump on some of our major blessings in life. I have always said that you have to have a "test" before you can have a "testimony", so put down the pride and become humble before the Lord.

What really inspires me about people like Bishop Brazier, is because they live by the "Keeping it Real" rule. I like for people to make it plain and simple, with no sugar coating when they give there testimony. "Keeping it Real" is the spiritually raw version of the story that tells me where you've been and where you going. I can't be encouraged by people who have inherited all of their blessings and never had to struggle with or for anything. People who keep it real tell how they made it over. They are the ones who will be a blessing because they are truthful. When you keep it real with others you are keeping it real with yourself. It provides a strong sense of deliverance for you and the person you are speaking and witnessing to.

Expectancy

I have been staying prayerful about my dreams and goals. I found out that through prayer, the Lord will unveil the things that He wants you to do. I believe in order to know what God expects of you, is to be prayerful and stay faithful. The Bible says, "Pray without ceasing". (1 Thessalonians 5:17) When I pray, I don't pray for just my dreams but for the dreams of the discouraged, the brokenhearted, and the hopeless. God is so awesome and I've come to realized that my dreams won't come to pass if I don't learn how to fully trust in Him. When I finally became submissive to the Lord, it allowed me to become more humble with a teachable spirit. I was able to learn how to trust (in Him and others who He sends my way) and become honest with myself by using discretion when speaking about my dreams. I'm praying for new opportunities and blessings to arise. I'm praying for favor, guidance and direction. I pray that as the Lord continues to shine over me that I'll be humble as I go higher in His abundant grace. I have a spirit of expectancy and in due time I will be able to birth my dreams into existence.

I've come to realize that taking action on your dream is very necessary. It's the next move on the "Chess" board of "Life". We must continue to stay focused on our dreams and all the positive things that are aligned with it. We have to learn not to settle for less and not to give into our setbacks. I sometimes think about all the dreams of the past that have been washed away. Every life that vanishes on this earth had a dream or two that never came to life. Life is so very short. How can you sit on a dream and not let it flourish into reality? Whatever we desire in our hearts should be displayed to others. We should be using the talents and gifts the Lord has given us and follow our hearts and dreams. Leave a legacy for your family to be proud of.

Lisha R. Williams

Dreams Passing Through

I spoke about how amazed I was by my thoughts and the level of confidence in myself to achieve when reading my Dream Journal. I realized that most of my discouragement came from fear, rejection and low self-esteem of the past. At one moment I felt as if I were on the top of a mountain's peak and then the next moment I felt I was at valley's low.

I believe that one of my biggest discouragements was obvious. I put my living situation, my finances and words of doubt from others in front of my dreams, which blocked my vision of success. I could only see the shadow of my dream because there wasn't a reflection of possibilities and opportunities for me to see. You can think thoughts of hope until doubt shows up or as my pastor would say, "When fear knocked on the door, faith answered and no one was there." You must overcome your fear of failure, defeat and low self-esteem.

One way to encourage yourself is to look at what your dream is. Decide today that you are going to take the leap of faith to make your dream possible. Think of the people who will benefit from your dream. Think of the people who care about you and want to see you achieve, like your kids, your parents, etc. Think of these things and shout "Hallelujah" because your backbone will begin to strengthen, your shoulders will become squared and your head will be lifted. Stand tall because the source of your strength is coming from the Lord.

Chapter 4

BELIEVE LITTLE OF WHAT YOU SEE AND NONE OF WHAT YOU HEAR

Be aware of those who approach you with crystal ball information. They are impostures because prophets are people who are sent by God to direct the path of His people. Prophets are not to be confused with the witchcraft involving crystal balls, zodiac signs and numbers. True prophets would never make "a profit" for what God has ordained them to do. It's a work from the Lord and for His kingdom.

God is not a magician and He doesn't make things complex like a puzzle that you need to piece everything together. He will supply all of your needs according to His riches and glory. (Phil. 4:19) This is a promise that God has given us so that we won't have to go out seeking and searching everywhere for things to come alive. When the Lord sends a messenger (or a prophet) you will feel their anointing of the Holy Spirit, which will give you confirmation. Even Paul had to remind Timothy in 1 Timothy 4:14 "to not neglect the gift [dream], which was given to him through a prophetic message..." As stated earlier, staying focused is the key to following your dreams and doing what the Lord God has called you to do.

KEEP ON LIVING

My grandmother always tells me to "keep on living" and "laugh to keep from crying". I was known for being the weeper of the family, not because I was the youngest of four, but it would give me a sense of comfort when I cried. That was only until I learned to laugh at my situation instead of crying about it. The mountain of defeat, failure, insecurities, low self-esteem, etc isn't bigger than the God we serve. The Word of God states that laughter is the greatest antidote to any circumstance or problem one could ever have, "A merry heart doeth good like a medicine: but a broken spirit drieth the bones." (Prov.17:22) Even Proverbs 15:13 says, "A merry heart maketh a cheerful countenance: but by sorrow of the heart the spirit is broken." This makes a lot of sense and it explains why it takes more muscles to frown then to smile.

When I began laughing at my circumstances, I began to feel relaxed because I know that I can cast my cares to the Lord, for He cares for me. (1 Peter 5:7) The enemy sends things your way because prophecies have already gone forth on your behalf. The enemy wants to kill it, steal it and (or) destroy it. You must remember that blessings are near when troubles arise because as the old cliché' goes, "misery loves company".

Laughing at your problems is easier said then done and it really sounds like a crazy thing to do. Yet this is what the Bible tells us and this is how we are to handle our enemies, with the act of kindness. We are not to allow the flesh to override the spirit with foolish talk. Kindness is the best weapon to kill off any infectious bacteria of defeat, failure, insecurities, gossip and fear. The weapons of our warfare are not carnal (or physical), but mighty through God to the pulling down of strong holds. (2 Cor. 10:4) Go ahead and laugh at the person who's laughing at you and your dreams, you're the one that's going to get the last laugh. If God has embedded this dream in you, even the devil in hell can't take it from you. You have the ability to walk out on faith and do what so many where afraid to do; that's to make your dream a reality. That's why it is so important to hold on to your faith and never let it go. I must reiterate that as many times as I can because you will be surprised how defeated some people can become on a daily basis. They have heard so many negative things either spoken over their life or over their dreams, to the point they can't get the concept of walking by faith and not by sight. (2 Cor 5:7)

One of my mentors, Kirby Jones, is the author of "Silence the Naysayers", one of the most outstanding books on faith and moving forward. In his book, he discusses how and why there is no weapon that's formed against you that will prosper. (Isaiah 54:17) One of the biggest weapons out there is the weapon of the tongue. The tongue has hurt so many people because of what comes from it. Despite the obvious germs, the germs of words that we speak are just as gross and disgusting. How can you bless and curse someone from the same tongue? Well, James 3:8 says that the tongue can't be tamed by man because it's an unruly (or restless) evil and filled with deadly poison. Verses 9 and 10 in New International Version (NIV) continues by saying that, "With the tongue we praise the Lord and Father, and with it we curse men, who have been made in God's likeness. Out of the same mouth come praise and cursing...this should not be."

So here's your homework, believe little of what you see and none of what you hear, laugh to keep from crying and learn to silence the naysayer.

Lisha R. Williams

Why should your dreams be outrageous?

We serve the Lord with faith through praise and worship. We believe that He will bless us with the desires of our hearts and supply our needs because He says so in His Word. Why do we do this? It's because He is Jehovah Jireh (My Provider) and El Shaddai (the God who's more than enough), so it gives us confidence to dream big because we know that our God blesses in abundance. The blessings that God has for you are already in order.

I have faith in my dreams that they will come to pass, as long as I stay within God's plan for my life. The dreams that I have are big, but it's nothing compared to what God has in store for me. When you dream of success, you actually feel that you can do it, even when all the odds are against you. So why is this feeling that we have temporary? Why does it feel that our desires come and go? It's the low scores and ratings that we give ourselves after our self-evaluation. We tell ourselves that we can't without even giving it a try.

Do you believe that your dreams are outrageous? You should believe that not only are they outrageous but they are the wackiest, craziest dreams you have ever dreamt. Dream big and move into your destiny. You are more than a stay-at-home mom, a soccer mom, a homemaker, a student, an average teenager, an employee...you are a dreamer, an inventor and moreover a child of a King.

What am I Looking For?

Honestly, there are times that I can feel like a complete failure or sometimes I just feel like I'm in the way and a bother to others. There are days when I feel like I'm trapped in a small box and there is no way out. I'm always excited about new ideas but when things don't work out, I become depressed and I can't even aim for Plan B. In the past, I've been known to give up easily and even in my Dream Journal I can see that I write down every excuse to why I can't continue on. It's just natural to have these types of feelings, though when we learn to sit down and ask ourselves, "What am I looking for?" we can clear our minds, take deep breaths and think things over.

Where do you go when there is no money in sight? Where do you go to find a peace of mind in the middle of chaos? Where can you find comfort in the midst of a storm? Jesus is who I turn to for help. He is not a crutch but comforter. Many who don't believe in Christ have a tendency to knock those who do believe in Him and what He is capable of doing. This is what makes things difficult in a Christian walk. ...Yet I still find my way back into His arms.

I would get into these pity parties and begin to feel sorry for myself. I would often wonder to myself, "where am I going in life...am I just another big disappointment to God?" Leave those types of questions in the bottomless pit of darkness to which they come from. Only the devil can cause you to act like that; talk like that. Say to yourself, "I am blessed and highly favored with God and I am the head and not the tail." Speak life to yourself until it takes root. Let the Holy Spirit take over you until it settles in your heart and mind that your dreams are in the hands of the Lord God. That's why God's ways are not like our ways and His thoughts are not like our thoughts. (Isaiah 55:8)

People, who believe in God, the Father, should also believe in the Son, Jesus Christ. When believing in the Son of God, you believe in the benefits that come with the plan of salvation. You will begin to believe in the power of prayer, anointing, favor and much more. So when it feels as if your back is up against the wall and that you are a failure, trust in God and all His righteousness. Man will fail you every time but God's love is everlasting, His promises are true.

Chapter 5

THROWING IN THE VOWEL

Everyone has a sense of defeat when obstacles come. They only come when you are reaching the point of your breakthrough, whether it's financial, healing or deliverance. Remember that when the wall of all your obstacles surface, just call on the Lord for the wall to be demolished. Obstacles are nothing more than stumbling blocks sent by the enemy to get you off course; when you are about to be blessed, be mindful not to share the news of your blessings with the world because most people are visual. They want to see the hand of God moving in your life for themselves. Let them know that the prayers of the righteous avail much. (James 5:16) Let them see the results of your prayers and fasting, your faith and beliefs. They have to see it in order to believe it.

When obstacles come your way, don't give up and don't give in. You have the power to break the barrier of defeat. You have the power to stand tall and say, "Yes, I can". It's all up to you because when you put your trust in God, you'll realize that you can do all things through Christ who strengthens you. (Phil. 4:13) The source of your strength comes from the Lord and God has provided you with the peace that passes all understanding. You have the power through the anointing of Christ to change your thought pattern. Change the way you think of yourself and your dreams. Face your fear of defeat. Challenge yourself to go out and do what God has called you to do. Don't throw in the towel but throw in a vowel and begin speaking blessings over your life.

Able	*You're able to conquer any level of defeat.*
Encouraged	*You are your biggest encouragement.*
Idealist	*You have the idea, which is the blueprint of your dream*
Opinion	*You have an opinion [option] to alter your dream.*
Unique	*You are to be unique and dream big. Don't follow what others say or do.*

When you throw in the vowel, you are being blessed every time because you are speaking blessings over your life and encouraging yourself to continue to push. When you face adversity or obstacles, remember to be bold and stand strong. Hold on to the unchanging Word of God.

Don't let anyone look down on you because you are young, but set an example for the believers in speech, in life, in love, in faith and in purity. (1 Timothy 4:12)

Paul's letter to Timothy was about instruction and building up confidence. Timothy was young but wise beyond his years. He knew that he was called but just needed direction and understanding in the role of leadership. He wanted to put his best foot forward but he knew that there were certain guidelines that he needed to follow in order to be successful in what God was calling him to do. It was a dream of his to do a great work for the Lord and starting out in the ministry is never easy. So this is why Paul felt led to give Timothy a boost by being his mentor and confidant.

Timothy wasn't the only young person in the Bible who was intimidated by his age. Jeremiah who is known for his statement, "I do not know how to speak, I am only a child" (Jer. 1:6), was one of the many people that God used through prophecy to lead the future generations through the destruction of nations up until the coming of Christ. Jesus was twelve when he wandered off in Jerusalem, only to find that he was in the synagogue asking questions and gaining knowledge, which was unfamiliar to the Jewish teachers. (Luke 2:42-47) Young Jabez, who was more honorable than his brothers, cried out to God and asked for a blessing that no man could take from his heart. (1 Chron. 4-10) The young shepherd boy David, who killed the giant Philistine Goliath, became king. Countless other young people who sought God first, gained wisdom and was blessed beyond their dreams. If these ordinary individuals can be used by God for extraordinary things, what makes any young person today believe they can't achieve the same and more?

When something is so bold and alive in spirit, you can't get it out of your mind or away from your heart. That's why you must pray on what it is that He wants you to do. Let God reveal a new thing to you; let Him shake it up, stir it up and place it on your path toward righteousness. I don't have a doubt in my mind that God doesn't want to see His children blessed but you must gain the wisdom in order to sustain such a blessing He has in store for you. Many nights I would cry myself to sleep because I knew what I wanted; I could see the vision of my dream over and over again. Sadly, I just couldn't grab a hold on to it. There were obstacles of fear, depression, failure and defeat, which lurked about me to the point that I felt like giving up before I even tried. It wasn't until I prayed to God to give me wisdom and guidance. I needed for Him to show me the way to where I needed to go; where He wanted me to go. I prayed for the Lord to use me just as He did Jeremiah and to send me a mentor as He did with Timothy. I desired so much from the Lord and I knew that it wouldn't be easy.

I know that I live in an era where many don't care about God and some don't even believe that He exists, but the Lord is enlarging my territory in the presence of my enemies. I trust Him in every way.

Be Encouraged

Keep your heart humble and always remember to be thankful.

Life has so much to offer and I know you feel that you have suffered.

But God has a plan for you and you must follow it.

You are precious to Him and you are indeed worth it.

You are more than a conqueror, believe me it is true.

Proof is written in Romans 8: 28-32.

God's has blessed you in so many different ways.

He was there yesterday and again with you today.

There's no need to give up hope,

Faith lies ahead.

There's no need to give up joy,

Sadness is death and death is dead.

Remember to smile because God will bring you out.

The miracles that He has prepared will make you shout.

He's a way-maker and He has healing in his wings.

Joy will come in the morning and He will change everything.

The struggle will soon be over but remember not to complain.

God is a healer and He will take away your frustration and pain.

Lisha R. Williams

Chapter 6

BE WILLING TO GIVE IN ORDER TO RECEIVE

When you do a good deed for someone, don't expect to be recognized for it. Let the recognition come spontaneously and give from the heart. The way to receive is to give and the key to giving is to be happy about it. For God loves a cheerful giver. (2 Cor 9:7) In order to gain, you must give!

Scenario 1

I was walking downtown Chicago when I noticed a homeless woman who was pregnant and sitting on the bare concrete. She was very malnourished and I didn't have much money, only two dollars to get on the bus and about $1.75 in coins. I felt horrible because I didn't have anything more to give and I wanted to help her. So I quietly walked up to her and gave her all the money I had, hoping for the best for her. She looked so feeble and I felt so helpless.

The young lady looked as if she was due to deliver at anytime but I wanted so desperately to know her story. Did she runaway? Was she abused? What happen? Her eyes were half shut and her lips were dry and chapped. Her hair was so dirty that it didn't even look blonde anymore. All I could do at that point was to pray for her. I had encountered homeless people on many occasions but nothing hit home like this woman. I could see her fear and her struggle to fight. I wondered what her dream was ten years prior to her current living situation.

I have always had a heart for the homeless and less fortunate. I always feel so useless when I can't give more than what I can and it's true that there are many impostures out there, but we have been given Godly wisdom and a spirit of discernment. Sometimes you can't pick the needles from the haystack but that's for the Lord to determine who's who as He judges our actions toward the ones that seek our help. When I gave my last to the young woman, I wasn't expecting anything in return. I was just hoping that I could be of some assistance to someone in need.

Scenario 2

On another trip downtown, I passed by a homeless man digging through the garbage for some food. I had just left a restaurant, where I barely touched my food because it was just so much. So I had the waiter wrap it up for take-out. When I saw the homeless man and I looked down at my food, without any hesitation I gave him my carry-out. When I handed him the food, he was so startled by the gesture. I wondered when was the last time this man saw a smile, heard the words "God bless you" and was given food to eat. It wasn't a holiday and it wasn't for recognition. I knew that this man was hungry and I fed him.

For I was hungry and you gave me something to eat, I was thirsty and you gave me something to drink, I was a stranger and you invited me in, I needed clothes and you clothed me, I was sick and you looked after me, I was in prison and you came to visit me.
(Matt. 25: 35-36 NIV)

I receive the greatest joy seeing others happy. When I gave my very last to the homeless woman, two days later someone had sacrifice their last to buy me lunch. When I gave my food away to the homeless man, a month or so later I had forgotten to bring my lunch to work. One of my co-workers, Linda, gave me her lunch because she wasn't hungry. I wasn't expecting any of these things to happen but it did and I was forever grateful.

I look at people who have a cold-heart toward the homeless, the less fortunate, the shut-in and even the elderly. I see people who are cruel to their neighbors and co-workers; little do they understand the effects of karma. What goes around comes around and you reap what you sow. How can they want anything from God when they can't even love their neighbor? It is always better to give than to receive. The Word tells us in Proverbs 28:27 (NIV) that "he who gives to the poor will lack nothing, but he who closes his eyes to them receives many curses."

I mentioned these two stories because a lot of people do good deeds for others to be recognized and rewarded. What I did for those two homeless people were things that I did from the heart; not expecting to be seen or rewarded. The greatest reward can only come from the Lord. No one can bless you like He can.

GIVE FROM THE HEART NOT FOR THE RECOGNITION

During my teen years, I really didn't get the concept of the benefits to reaping and sowing. The preacher would always aggravate me when he would talk about tithes and offerings and of course being a teenager you think that you know everything anyway. I didn't understand that I was holding up my own blessing with this negative attitude I had about harvesting.

II Chronicles 31:5, the Israelites gave a tenth of everything they had from grain to oil and wine and honey. These were there contributions for worship that were made under the law. Though what I noticed about the entire chapter is that everyone contributed to Lord, even in leadership. What inspire them to want to give? Was it because it was order by Hezekiah to do so? No, it says that the Israelites generously gave the first fruits of everything. So why do we complain about giving? There is no reason to complain but this is the purpose for being a cheerful giver. I had to realize that God is only asking for 10% oppose to a waiter's tip at a restaurant for 15%. I had to come to the understanding that God doesn't ask for much.

I only mention this because I was struggling with my finances. I was praying for God to bless me financially and to help me manage my funds. I was asking all of this from the Lord but I was doing what He asked of me. I was having big financial difficulties, all due to disobedience to the Lord God.

I continued with this thought process that I wasn't going to give my money to the preacher to blow on a fancy car or a big house. What arrogance? I was young and rebellious; I felt that I wasn't going to allow myself to fall short of a church prank. Little did I know that the money I was earning every two weeks didn't belong to me, it belonged to the Lord and He gave it to me just so that I could give a tenth back to Him.

..."*bless me indeed and enlarge my territory, that your hand will be with me to keep me from evil so that I may not cause pain. Amen*"
(1 Chronicles 4:10)

I finally got down on my knees and asked the Lord to deliver me from all my troubles. When I finished praying, the Lord spoke to my spirit and said, sow $100 to the ministry. I only had $100 to my name and I was skeptical at first but I realized the flesh was trying to override the spirit, though I did it by faith and faith alone. Anyone who knows about faith can tell you that it's the most radical thing that one could ever experience. I immediately sent my last $100 to the ministry; no later than a week later, the Lord had blessed me with $1,000 from my mentor, Pastor Godfrey. Pastor Godfrey didn't know what I was going through financially or the spiritual battle that I was having about reaping and sowing the harvest. The Lord blessed me through Pastor Godfrey because I was obedient to Him. I reaped what I sowed and it was returned to me double. When I got that $1,000, I prayed over it and sent another $100 to the ministry. The Lord challenged me again and tested my level of faith. He said to me, "you owe your sister $800, give her $800." I was stunned because I was planning to pay my bills with that money. Yet I was obedient to the Lord and I gave my sister the $800. Three days later, I received an important e-mail regarding my investment plan from my job that I had quit three months prior. When I opened the e-mail I was overwhelmed with joy to see that my former boss contributed $800 to my 401(k) plan.

God is awesome and I believe what the Lord says in His Word. The Lord wants to bless His children but in order to receive; you have got to be able to give. His Word is true. "God is not a man, that He should lie, nor a son of man, that He should change His mind. Does He speak and then not act? Does he promise and not fulfill?

I have received a command to bless; He has blessed, and I cannot change it." (Numbers 23:19-20 NIV)

Scenario 3

"A customer walks in a convenience store with the intentions of making this a quick, in and out visit. He figured that his one item of beer shouldn't take longer than ten minutes. So he decided to go to the express line for those who have 15 items or less. The man became irritated with the woman in line ahead of him. She is short a few dollars but she really needed to buy the diapers, milk and a small tube of baby ointment for her baby. She was a young mother, not quite sure about the age, but she was extremely embarrassed for not having enough to buy these items for her new-born baby.

The man became so impatient and made the young lady feel so nervous as she rushed and searched for coins at the bottom of her purse. Finally the manager walked up to her and said, "Miss, don't worry about a thing. Your bill has been paid in full." The woman looked puzzled but she was very gracious to the manager. He smiled at her and helped with her bag. The man in line wanted to know how come he had to pay and the lady didn't. So he went and asked the manager why such a generous offer was made, the manager just simply replied, "She has favor."

When the Lord blesses you, He comes when you least expect Him to. He even blesses you in the presence of your enemy. David says in Psalms 23:5, "You [Lord] prepare a table before me in the presence of my enemies." The bill that was paid for the woman was made by an anonymous source, a cheerful giver who was not expecting to be recognized. The Lord touched someone's heart to show this young lady favor.

Chapter 7

The Enemy Still Can't Stop Me

I woke up this morning with praise on my lips
Head tilted back, hands on my hips
I jumped up and down and shouted unto Him
Jehovah Jireh, El Shaddai, Elohim
I danced like David, I sang like Paul and Silas
Victorious, Righteous...Oh nothing can't stop this
I just wanted magnify and glorify my Lord
'Cause I have so much to be thankful for
He's been so good to me; words can't express
He's delivered me from all the devil's mess
I prayed for angels to be my protection
I asked the Lord for His direction
I prayed for those who are going through
Which are my loved ones, that means you
I bind-up every evil, demonic force sent by the enemy
And every negative thought from his adversaries
It ain't nothing he can do, you believe me
The enemy still can't stop me.

Every morning I wake up with a smile on my face, knowing that this is the day that the Lord has made and I shall rejoice and be glad in it. (Psalms 118:24 KJV) I am always so thankful that the Lord sees fit to allow me to see another day. Do you realize that when you wake up in the morning with life, health and strength, that it's a gift sent down from heaven to you...everyday? That's a gift that only the Lord can give you. Beyond your medication, your vitamins, your energy drink, your coffee, etc only the Lord can provide you with this gift of life. I think about those days when I would tell someone that I wasn't having a good day. How can I say something so absurd, so early in the morning and the day hadn't even begun? I just prophesied doom over the rest of my day for no apparent reason. I have to look forward to seeing great things and experiencing unexpected blessings. Is anything too hard for God? Absolutely not! So this is why the enemy can't stop you from moving forward and conquering your dreams.

Many of you who are reading this book feel encouraged to dream on and make a You-Turn on life. Some of you are still afraid to soar like the eagles and settle on the mountain's peak. Let me tell you this, you have reached chapter seven. This is the final chapter and the number seven represents completion. You should be excited about making a You-Turn because the devil can't stop you from getting ahead. The Word of the Lord says this:

"If I had cherished sin in my heart, the Lord would not listen. Jesus Christ is the same yesterday and today and forever. Let us then approach the throne of grace with confidence, so that we may receive mercy and find grace to help us in our time of need. Be careful to follow every command I am giving you today, so that you may **live** *and* **increase** *and may* **enter** *and* **possess** *the land the Lord promised on oath to your forefathers. Remember how the Lord your God led you all the way in the desert these forty years; to humble you and to test you in order to know what was in your heart, whether or not you would keep His commands. He humbled you causing you to hunger and then feeding you manna, which neither you nor your fathers had known, to teach you that man does not live on bread alone but on every word that come from the mouth of the Lord."*
(Psa. 66:18, Heb. 13:8, Heb. 4:16 & Deut. 8:1-3 NIV)

Go ahead and make a You-Turn on the road of life.
Dream the impossible dream because God is the possible God.

The You – Turn

About the Author

Lisha Ranelle Williams is the Founder and President of Angels N D'Skys Organization, a ministry designed to help teens and young adults strive for excellence. Lisha was born on December 8, 1981 in Chicago, IL and is the youngest of three sisters.

When Lisha first began this ministry, in the year 2000, its main goal was to assist young people in believing that they could achieve their goals against all odds. Lisha's first book "A Teen's Perspective" spoke of the struggles she faced during her school years, specifically during high school. Lisha was a senior in high school when the Columbine shootings happen on April 20, 1999. This was the incident that prompted her to writing books of hope and encouragement. The first book, "A Teen's Perspective", consisted of poetry, history and short stories. It was a big motivation to young people and a big part of who Lisha was.

Some of Lisha's biggest role models are Langston Hughes, Frederick Douglass, Maya Angelou, Gwendolyn Brooks, The Williams' Bros. and Lena Horne, just to name a few. Lisha's talent for writing began when she was only nine years old, from writing poetry, to songs, to plays and so much more, Lisha has always enjoyed writing. Although, writing wasn't the only art the young author gripped a hold to. She also danced at Mayfair Academy of Fine Arts in Chicago where she began her training with ballet, tap and modern jazz. She later took up the interest for acting with a special program at Columbia College in Chicago and was featured in two gospel plays with B.A. Blessing Productions titled "A Christmas Miracle" and "Seeking for a Mate". Lisha began writing songs and contributing music for various plays and productions.

Lisha is looking forward to writing her next book. She hopes that all of her books will encourage and uplift many to dream the impossible dream with making the necessary You-Turns in life to make those dreams come alive.

www.ingramcontent.com/pod-product-compliance
Lightning Source LLC
Chambersburg PA
CBHW032030040426
42448CB00006B/797